DEGAS

By GIOVANNI CARANDENTE

AVENEL BOOKS

NEW YORK

Degas © MCMLXXIX by Fabbri Editori, Milan, Italy
English Translation Copyright © by Fabbri Editori, Milan, Italy
All Rights Reserved
First U.S. Edition published 1979 by Avenel Books
distributed by Crown Publishers Inc.
225 Park Avenue South, New York, N.Y. 10003
Printed in Italy by Gruppo Editoriale Fabbri, Milan

b   c   d   e   f   g   h   i

Translation by STEPHEN SARTARELLI

Library of Congress Cataloging in Publication Data
Degas, Hilaire Germain Edgar, 1834-1917.
Degas.
1. Degas, Hilaire Germain Edgar, 1834-1917.
I. Carandente, Giovanni.
ND553.D3A4 1979 759.4 78-71507
ISBN 0-517-27790-5

The nineteenth century in Europe was a period of rapid modernization and intense transformation, affecting all aspects of life. A new view of the world was needed, and the task of creatively capturing and conveying the ongoing changes became the work of the artist, as it does in all such periods. It was the role of the late nineteenth century painters to create new modes of expression that would incorporate the genius of the past and infuse it with the talent of the present, and it was Edgar Degas who integrated the classical approach to art with the revolutionary techniques of Impressionism perhaps better than any of his contemporaries.

Degas was born in Paris on july 19, 1834. His given name was Hilaire Germain Edgar de Gas, and he signed his paintings that way until 1873, when he began using the name by which he is known today. His father was Auguste de Gas, a banker who was also actively interested in the arts. Auguste was born in Naples, Italy, the son of a Frenchman exited at the time of the French Revolution. He later returned to Paris and married a young Creole from New Orleans whose family had once emigrated to America. She died when Edgar was thirteen years old, and thus his artistic education was guided by his father. The two often visited the museums of Paris, and when Edgar was eighteen Auguste provided him with an art studio of his own after the young man's brief and unsuccessful attempt at studying law.

At nineteen Degas had already produced impressive copies of the paintings of the Old Masters that were in the Louvre and the Cabinet des Dessins. In his sketchbooks of this period there are pages inspired by Ingres and the Renaissance masters, as well as many delicate self-portraits. At twenty Degas studied under the tutorship of Louis Lamothe, a pupil and devoted admirer of Ingres. It was during this period that the foundation of what would become Degas's superb draftsmanship was laid. Within a year Degas enrolled in the Ecole des Beaux-Arts.

In 1854 Degas made his first trip to Italy, where he visited (with) his paternal grandfather, in Naples. He journeyed in 1856 to Florence, where he stayed with the Bellelli family (his father's sister, Laura, was now the Baroness Bellelli). His third and most productive trip to Italy was in 1858, when he visited Perugia, Assisi, Viterbo, and Orvieto, as well as Rome, and once again Naples and Florence. At Orvieto he produced several drawings of the frescoes of Luca Signorelli.

While in Florence he began the celebrated "The Bellelli Family", a work he had been planning for some time. These trips to Italy decidely influenced the style in which Degas painted. There he was exposed to the fifteenth-century Italians, such as Botticelli, whom he particularly admired.

From 1860 to 1865 Degas dedicated himself to painting historical subjects to the exclusion of all else. "The Misfortunes of the City of Orléans", which was exhibited at the official Salon of 1865, was typical of the work of this period. In 1861 Degas met Edouard Manet. Manet introduced him to the circle of young Impressionist painters who frequently met at the Café Guerbois in Paris. The café was the gathering place for the creative artists whose energies were bursting upon the Parisian scene at that time; the writers Emile Zola and Edmond Duranty joined Cézanne, Renoir, Sisley, Monet, and Pisarro there weekly, usually on Thursdays, and discussions were volatile.

When Prussia advanced on Paris during 1870-71, Degas and many of his colleagues served in an artillery division until the armistice was signed. He then left for Valpincons to stay at the home of some friends. In the meantime Gustave Courbet, newly elected people's commissioner for the arts and an exponent of realism, was revolutionizing the concepts of the Parisian art world.

When Degas returned to Paris in 1872, he was introduced to the Opéra world by a musician friend, Désiré Dehau, who later appeared frequently in Degas's opera paintings. While the opera house was under reconstruction as a result of war damages, the school of dance met in the rue Le Pelletier, and this was the setting Degas depicted in his first painting on what was to be a favorite and famous subject – dancers – "Le Foyer de la Danse à l'Opéra de la rue Le Pelletier".

In 1872-73 Degas made a six-month voyage to New Orleans, where he visited with his American relatives and stayed at the home of his brother, René. When he returned to Paris, he rejoined his colleagues and played an active role in the preparation of the first Impressionist exhibition at the Durand-Ruel gallery in 1874. He also met novelist Edmond de Goncourt, who visited Degas at his studio and later wrote enthusiatically of the meeting in his diary.

In 1881 Degas created "A Dancer at the Age of Fourteen" – his first sculpture – which he carved in wax and dressed in tutu, corset, and silk shoes. This was the first in the long series of works in which he sought to delineate the expressive movements of ballerinas.

As early as 1870, during military service, Degas had complained of difficulty with his eyesight, and it was this problem that led him to work in pastels. Despite a worsening condition, however, his experiments with technique became more complex, and in his last years of active work he integrated such disparate methods as oils, pastels, tempera, and wax.

In 1886 Degas returned to Naples and also visited Spain, and in 1889 he returned to Spain and journeyed from there to Le Havre and Dieppe. At the eignt and final exhibition of the Impressionists in 1886, Degas exhibited a celebrated series of nudes – "women bathing, washing, drying, rubbing down, combing their hair and having it combed". His sight was already seriously impaired when he journeyed to Montauban the following year to see the works of Ingres, the master who had influenced him so greatly. Shortly after his return he retreated to his home at Saint-Valéry-sur-Somme, surrounding himself with the works of Ingres, Delacroix and Courbet. There he lived out the final years of his life in such seclusion that little is known about him during this period. He died on September 27, 1917, at a time when the world was gripped by such deep human tragedy that there was hardly any thought given to the evolution of art forms.

3

"To this date, he has known better than anyone else how to capture the spirit of modern life".

Edmond de Goncourt, 1874

Young Spartans at exercise - London, National Gallery

Born into a wealthy family, Hilaire Germain Edgar de Gas embodied manners and style of the nineteenth-century aristocracy. Although he was brought up in a cosmopolitan atmosphere, Degas was devoid of bohemian attitudes. On the contrary, he was refined, disdainful, sometimes caustic and even pompous. Many thought him the most unpredictable of the masters of the Impressionist movement.

An early and close friend of Manet, degas was not at the outset of his work innovative as his artist friend was. He had an inquisitive mind and a fertile imagination, but his desire for knowledge seemed almost in conflict with his secluded way of living. Perhaps because of these opposing tendencies, he alternated between the style of Ingres and the study of the Renaissance masters during his formative years. Yet this ambivalence was positively expressed in a facility that enabled him to move from classical paintings to family portraits, from historical and heroic scenes to fresh visions of contemporary life.

In all Degas's works there is a precision that is personally his, a uniqueness in composition, modeling and color, and this can be found even in the earliest works that are also rich with the influence of the Renaissance masters as well as of Ingres and sometimes Delacroix. His family background at first directed him toward the more traditional Parisian artists, often referred to as the "Ingrists". His first studies were with Louis Lamothe, one of Ingres's most devoted and rigorous followers.

During this apprenticeship, however, Degas came to realize that the tradition available to him in the halls of the Louvre, represented by such painters as Leonardo da Vinci, Dürer, Holbien and other masters could provide a wealth of inspiration and instruction that he could assimilate into his own creative vision.

He discovered that in addition to the strong influence of Ingres, the nineteenth-century Parisian climate was alive with the romanticism of Delacroix, the realism of Courbet, the contented pastoral scenes of Corot and the naturalness of the *plein air* painters of the Barbizon school. All these worked their subtle influences on Degas and combined with his exposure to the

5

Woman drying herself - Chicago, by courtesy of the Art Institute, Mr. and Mrs. M.A. Ryerson collection

Pollaiuolo and Mantegna. He regarded the composure of Renaissance art more favorably than the elegance of the mannerists, and only later in his work did he turn to the variations of color and light characteristic of Venetian art.

In 1861 Degas met Manet while copying a Velazquez in the Louvre. From the outset of their friendship the two artists discovered they had much in common: their attitudes toward life, their spiritual dispositions and their similarly wealthy backgrounds. It took little time for them to come to an appreciation of each other's work, and they shared a strong respect for creative freedom, even though Manet did not agree with Degas's choice of subject. He frowned upon Degas's intricately detailed historical scenes, and the classical system of structure that was so prevalent in his work, even though Degas was incorporating in them lively and modern themes. Manet did, however, appreciate novel qualities in the now famous "The Bellelli Family". He admired the boldness of the composition and the facial expressions that reflect almost imperceptible moods of the family, as well as insight into their intimate domestic situation – the emotional distance between husband and wife.

Manet disapproved of Degas's historical scenes because he soundly rejected the practices of the Ecole des Beaux-Arts, which restricted itself to precise renditions of traditional themes. Yet in paintings of this period, such as "Young Spartans Exercising" (1860), Degas did not adhere to the strictly classical Greek figures. He painted instead the youths of Paris and Montmartre, who were short, muscular and looked at the world through melancholy eyes. With this sense of reality, Degas mitigated the pomposity of his subjects. He achieved similar effects in other paintings of this period, such as "Semiramis Founding Babylon" and "Daughter of Jefte". It is in these works, that Degas most vividly conveys the dictum of his mentor Ingres: "Make lines, young man, many lines, from life or from memory, and you will become a good artist". And so the purity of line in Degas's historical works united with the inner vitality of his realism. And while these early works did not bring him the fame of his later years, they do represent that transitional period of French art between Ingres and that which would be born at the Salon des Refusés in 1863.

Renaissance painters in Italy to produce a blending of tradition with innovation that burst forth on his later canvasses.

Degas thus begame the first precursor of modern art to draw from paintings of the fifteenth-century Italian painters known as the *quattrocentisti*. He especially concentrated on those artists who exalted the line as the principal figurative element – Botticelli,

Washer - women carrying linen - USA, private collection

It may be somewhat surprising, then, that when Degas exhibited for the first time at the official Salon of 1865, he leaned toward pleasing the traditional critics who two years before had raised such loud objections to "the scandal" of Manet's "Le déjeuner sur l'Herbe". Degas presented an elaborately classicist composition entitled "The Misfortunes of the City of Orléans", which did indeed please the critic very much.

As his diary revealed, Degas had decided early on the approach he intended to follow. The study of nature did not hold for him any particular importance insofar as "painting is an art of convention, and it is much more worth one's while to learn to draw from Holbein than from a landscape". For these reasons his principal preoccupation at this time remained that of discovering in each work a "living line, human and intimate", even though so many of his Parisian colleagues were leaving the city to paint nature's mutable appearances in a changing light.

Degas always stood somewhat aloof from the Impressionist's regard for the painting of landscapes as an entity in itself. He was not interested in it except as a background of his racing or figure scenes, and therefore was not so much concerned with capturing the changes of light outdoors. He was more interested in the craftmanship of the draftsman. After reading in his diaries his comments about how he wanted to depict contemporary life, one might say that he wanted to transfer the conceptions of the Impressionists to the inner city: to the windows of the bakeries and pastry shops, to the Café Chantant, to the ballerinas and the sidewalk cafés in the evening hours where "the street lamp's different nature reflects off the wine glasses", as he once wrote.

He did not, however, adhere strictly to these subjects, but applied his artistic vision to painting commonplace objects with the same vitality as human figures – for example "a corset just removed, which would still preserve the body's form". Degas was especially excited by the worlds of opera and ballet and by the field of Longchamps with its racehorses – and these were again and again the subjects of his canvasses. He was perhaps the most naturally eloquent poet to sing of the elegant world of the ballet. He celebrated in line and color the graceful ballerinas in all their moods and settings: as they danced on stage, stood in the fantasy-colored footlights or waited in the wings for the excitement of curtaincall applause. Capturing emotions – whether in excitement or calm – became one of the most delightful motifs of his art.

The theme of the ballerinas began with the celebrated "Le Foyer de la Danse à l'Opéra de la rue Le Pellietier", of 1872, a work that also displays an intriguing architectural complexity achieved through the diversity of the poses of the ballerinas. In the ballerina paintings Degas captured the essence of human movement as light and ethereal as was then conceivable. Even the portrait he painted in New Orleans that same year of his blind sister-in-law, Estelle, "Mme René de Gas", seems to show traces of that silver gauziness the artist had learned to love in the wings of the Opéra.

During his visit in Louisiana with his brother, René, he was seized with ideas for many new projects that were inspired by the exotic setting of New Orleans. But these quickly faded, as a letter he wrote to a friend reveals: "Art does not expand, it re-engages itself". And, indeed, by the time he sailed for home, all the ideas were reabsorbed into his meditative processes. "Those projects would have required ten lives if I had carried them out", he declared upon his return.

Yet he did capture a poignant remembrance of his sojourn in Louisiana in the painting "New Orleans Cotton Office" – a portrayal of the interior of his Uncle Musson's office filled with customers. It is a lively painting, in its architectural squaring effect as well as in the sharp portraiture of the persons depicted. It is therefore significant that this painting was given the title "Portraits in an Office" when it was shown at the Impressionist exhibit of 1876 in the Durand-Ruel gallery. The subtlety of its design could be called neoclassical, but the juxtaposition of colors (the white of the cotton, the newspapers, the books, the shirtsleeves of the cashier intently consulting the cash register, alternated with the grays) generates a rhythm previously unknown. Moreover, the clarity and simplicity of the representation make it living document of a vanished epoch of America that is today re-created in the cinema with much more ephemeral results.

Mary Cassatt at the Louvre - Philadelphia, Henry C. Mc. Ilhemy
collection

When Degas returned to France after this visit, he immersed himself in such poignantly realistic subjects as ''Rehearsal'' (1873), ''L'Absinthe'' (1876), ''Aux Ambassadeurs'' (1877) and the portrait of ''Diego Martelli'' (1879). In these works he gave himself free rein in composition and total freedom in the intense and vibrant use of color.

These slices of life, which are almost photographic, figure among the artist's greatest work because of their intense perception and psychological astuteness. When ''L'Absinthe'' was shown in London in 1893, it caused a memorable scandal.

Puritanical British critics accused Degas of wanting to exalt the depravity of bohemian life, but he believed he merely captured the realism of life as it was in Paris. Two friends of his posed for the painting – the engraver Desboutin and the actress Ellen Andrée and it was Degas's sensitivity that elevated the banal to the level of art.

In ''L'Absinthe'' the bold perspective of one angle of the sidewalk café La Nouvelle-Athènes at Place Pigalle is the same as that of the ''New Orleans Cotton Office'', but in contrast to the complexity of the office painting, ''L'Absinthe'' offers the disarming simplicity of life as it is for the less than successful.

In addition, the painting's tone reflects the influence that Japanese art was having on Degas. Degas had already sketched a Japanese print in the background of the portrait of his friend, Jacques James Tissot, several years earlier. And since then Japanese prints had become an integral part of the Parisian scene.

The café at Place Pigalle succeeded the Café Guerbois as the favorite meeting place of the Impressionists, and there they often gathered as sunset bathed the streets of Paris and the Lamplighters slowly began their rounds. Although Degas frequented the cafés where his colleagues passed their evenings, he remained detached, even aloof, from their artistic debates, keeping his own counsel. The writer Edmond Duranty, a regular member of the group as well as a close friend of Degas, remembered him as ''always preoccupied with his own ideas'' – which, he admitted, seemed a bit eccentric to the rest.

Duranty recounts that at the Café Guerbois friends ironically labeled Degas ''the inventor of social chiaroscuro''. The title no doubt was conferred because Degas expressed a desire to pursue an art that would appeal to the elect few rather than the common masses. Yet by other contemporaries he was called the ''master of contre-lumière». Indeed, few artists knew as he did how to create this effect and render so delicately the nuances of light and reflection.

After 1886, Degas withdrew more and more into himself. The worsening eye condition tormented him, and at times he was morose and depressed. His only exhibition after this was in 1892 at the Durant-Ruel gallery, where he presented a series of landscapes in pastels. This came as a surprise because of his previous attitude that landscapes had value only as backgrounds, even in his famous horseracing series.

With the failing of his eyesight, Degas prefered to work increasingly in pastels. The celebrated series of ''women bathing, washing, drying, rubbing down, combing their hair and having it combed» conveys best the artist's technique where the forms give way to the effects of light and color. In the soft outline made by the pastel, Degas was able to fuse the old fervor of the line with an Impressionistic pictorial effect. Every pastel stroke became an accent of color, and the role that this played in his completed oeuvre coincided with the goals of Impressionism. Degas's pastels took on the appearance of fireworks, and the frenzy of the light was converted into a luminous blossoming of color. The sureness of his inner eye, which could not be dimmed by the failure of his sight, transformed his experience and techniques into masterpieces that have not only withstood the test of time but have grown more lyrical and incandescent with the passage of years.

The strength and originality of his style, from its classical beginnings to its Impressionistic maturity, is acknowledged today by art lovers and critics alike. His contemporaries appreciated him for his ability to capture the quality of the life of his day – the time of Emile Zola, Guy de Maupassant, Edmond de Goncourt and Edmond Duranty. Today Degas's masterpieces are considered timeless expressions of ephemeral beauty captured forever, present and living for generations yet unborn.

Index of the illustrations

I - Self-portrait - 1854-1855 - Paris, Musée National du Louvre - *An early work, this dates from the artist's first trip to Italy. The influence of the Romantic portrait painters is clearly visible in the use of somber colors and in the treatment of the subject.*

II - René de Gas as a Child - 1855 - Collection of Mr. and Mrs. Paul Mellon - *Although Degas usually portrayed his models with a rapt, wistful expression, this portrait of his younger brother is particularly cheerful.*

III - Achille de Gas in the Uniform of a Cadet - 1856-1857 - Washington, D.C., National Gallery of Art, Chester Dale Collection - *This portrait of the artist's brother shows the neoclassical influence of Ingres and, at the same time, a romantic tendency toward the use of deep colors and somber expressions.*

IV - The Duke and Duchess of Morbilli - 1867 - Boston, The Museum of Fine Arts, gift of R. Treat Paine - *In the portrait of his sister and her italian husband. Edmondo Morbilli, the luminous background heightens the expressive qualities of the subjects.*

V - The Roman Beggarwoman - 1857 - Birmingham, Alabama, City Museum and Art Gallery - *In this realistic effort, the artist has used the example of the Old Masters to create a style that is unique and personal.*

VI - Henri Ronart in Front of His Factory - c. 1875 - Pittsburgh, Museum of Art, Carnegie Institute - *Henri Ronart, a close friend and admirer of the artist, introduced him to many leading artists and intellectuals of the day.*

VII - Portrait of Giovanna Bellelli - Rome, The Gualino Collection - *Degas did many preliminary studies of his young cousins, which culminated in the famous family portrait. Of them, this is the most complete; the model's sister, Giulia, is only outlined on the right.*

VIII - Semiramis Founding Babylon - 1861 - Paris, Musée National du Louvre - *Never completed, this work is one of a five-part series depicting historical scenes. The neoclassical influence is evident.*

IX - The Bellelli Family - 1860-1862 - Paris, Musée National du Louvre - *The importance of this painting as an innovation in portraiture is expressed in the artist's own words, by his desire "to portray people within the familiarity of their own natural surroundings", giving to their faces "the same sort of expressiveness that can be seen in their bodies".*

X - Woman with Chrysanthemums - 1865 - New York, Metropolitan Museum of Art, donated by Mrs. H.O. Havemayer, from her husband's collection - *Here Degas's typical portrait style is displayed: the subject is shown in her own environment, in a characteristic pose.*

 XI - The Laundress - 1869 - Private collection - *It was Degas's practice to make numerous studies of his subjects before completing the work. This unfinished canvas is an example of one of the various steps involved in the passage from idea to completed work.*

 XII-XIII - The Orchestra at the Opera - 1868-1869 - Paris, Musée National du Louvre - *Originally begun as a portrait of Désirée Dehau, the painting grew to encompass the entire theatrical ambience, in all its movement, spectacle, color and elegance.*

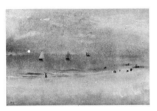 XIV - At the Seaside - 1869 - Paris, Musée National du Louvre, Cabinet des Dessins, Cliché des Musées Nationaux - *During 1869 Degas spent many hours sketching by the sea, attempting to reproduce in pastels the moist and briny luminosity of the French coast.*

 XV - Portrait of Hortense Valpinçon (detail) - 1869 - Minneapolis Institute of Arts - *Paul Valpinçon was a close friend of Degas. Edouard Valpinçon, Paul's father, had introduced the artist to Ingres. During a visit to the Valpinçon family, Degas painted Hortense in lively colors that give the painting a feeling of spontaneity.*

 XVI - Portrait of Léopold Levert - Private collection - *Throughout his career, Degas would turn again and again to the portrait form to express his fascination with people and the worlds they inhabited.*

 XVII - New Orleans Cotton Office - 1873 - Pau, France, Musee des Beaux-Arts - *Here Degas portrays his family and friends amid the stir and confusion of a Southern cotton market. His uncle Musson is examining cotton samples; his brother René is reading a newspaper; his older brother Achille leans against a window, while cashier John Livandais leafs through his accounts.*

 XVIII-XIX - Le Foyer de la Danse a l'Opéra de la Rue le Pelletier - 1872 - Paris, Musée National du Louvre - *The world of dance was a constant source of inspiration to Degas, as can be seen here in the delicate play of gold and silver lights, and the warm shades of ochre.*

 XX - Carriage at the Races - 1870-1873 - Boston, Museum of Fine Arts - *In addition to the world of the dance, the color and excitement of the race track inspired Degas. This masterly study of jockeys and sleek horses is one of his best.*

 XXI - At the Race Course (detail) - Paris, Musée National du Louvre - *Degas began painting horse races even before his friend Manet did. This composition makes subtle use of perspective and asymmetry to accentuate the feeling of motion.*

 XXII - Seated Dancer - 1874 - Paris, Musée National du Louvre, Cabinet des Dessins, Cliché des Musées Nationaux - *This sketch on blue paper is typical of Degas's use of the dance motif to analyze the lines of the body.*

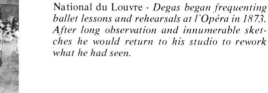 XXIII - The Dance Lesson - 1874 - Paris, Musée National du Louvre - *Degas began frequenting ballet lessons and rehearsals at l'Opéra in 1873. After long observation and innumerable sketches he would return to his studio to rework what he had seen.*

 XXIV - Dancer Seen from the Back - 1876 - Paris, Musée National du Louvre, Cabinet des Dessins, Cliché des Musées Nationaux - *This drawing, on glossy red paper, in ink and watercolors, is probably a study for one of the artist's many works on the dance lesson.*

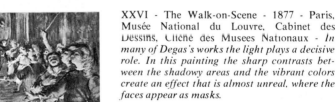 XXIV-XXV - Women Combing Their Hair - 1875-1876 - Washington, D.C., Phillips Collection - *Mixing oil with turpentine forces color to a clear essence, as opposed to the heavy, vivid effect of pastels. Here we can see how the technique invigorates an image, as it does in these subtle variations of the same human theme.*

 XXVI - The Walk-on-Scene - 1877 - Paris, Musée National du Louvre, Cabinet des Dessins, Cliché des Musees Nationaux - *In many of Degas's works the light plays a decisive role. In this painting the sharp contrasts between the shadowy areas and the vibrant colors create an effect that is almost unreal, where the faces appear as masks.*

XXVII - L'Absinthe - 1876 - Paris, Musée National du Louvre - *This famous* tableau vivant *reveals the influence of Japanese art in Degas, in the boldness of its perspective. The oblique lines of the table seem to anticipate the later "theater" paintings, and descend from the grand tradition.*

 XXVIII - Café Concert - 1876 - Washington, D.C., The Corcoran Gallery of Art, W. A. Clark Collection - *The striking contrasts—the diagonal lines of the stage, the movements caught and held as if by a camera lens—all contribute to making this pastel a masterwork in form and visual dynamics.*

 XXIX - Café Concert at Les Ambassadeurs - Lyon, Musée des Beaux-Arts - *This is one of Degas's finest renderings of theater life in Paris. He first did a monotype of the subject and then filled it in with pastels. The series of bright colors culminates in the backlit figure of the singer.*

 XXX-XXXI - The Rehearsal - 1877 - Glasgow Art Gallery and Museum, the Sir William Burrell Collection - *The first of Degas's "Foyer" paintings, in 1872, was in the classic style, but soon gave way to the Impressionistic technique, suffused and vibrating with light. This use of light and the juxtaposition of still with moving figures gives this work dynamic mobility.*

 XXXII - Ballerina with Fan - 1874 - Private collection - *This work is a result of the artist's many experiments in combining media, such as tempera, watercolor and oil, to develop new techniques.*

 XXXIII - Singer with Glove - 1878 - Cambridge, Massachusetts, the Fogg Art Museum, Harvard University, Gift of Maurice Wertheim - *The vividness of this pastel can be explained in part by the illumination of the face, the sharp contrasting of black and white in the footlights, and the intense sense of mobility in the woman's gesture.*

 XXXIV - Dancer on Stage - 1880 - Private collection - *Degas worked his dance motif in many different ways and with a variety of techniques. This painting is a combination of pastels with tempera, a mixture which enabled the painter to create unusual effects of illumination.*

 XXXV - The Ballet Rehearsal (detail) - New York, The Metropolitan Museum of Art, the Havemeyer Collection - *From the dance classes, Degas passed quickly on to studies of the dress rehearsals where, on stage, the dancer's graceful pliés are visible beyond the orchestra against the light.*

 XXXVI-XXXVII - On the Stage - Chicago, The late Potter Palmer Collection - *Using pastels, blurring outlines to give a sense of the ephemeral, enabled the artist to reproduce the delicate, fairy-like qualities of the romantic ballet.*

XXXVIII - The Trainers - 1880 - Private collection - *This race course scene is a unique study in spatial dimension, with innovational use of depth and perspective.*

 XXXIX - Jockeys in the Rain - 1881 - Glasgow Art Gallery and Museum - *This work in pastel shows the original way in which Degas portrayed exterior scenes. He achieved the harmonious balance of line by setting off different planes and perspectives against each other.*

 XL-XLI - Race Horses - 1885 - Private collection - *An unmistakable trait of Degas, exemplified by this pastel, is the way he crops figures and positions them to create the illusion of three dimensions, where foregrounds appear very near and backgrounds distant.*

 XLII - The Riders, or the Start of the Race - 1885 - *Movement is the real protagonist here. The energy of the horses are caught in this moment on canvas.*

 XLIII - Horse Jumping Over an Obstacle - Bronze, 1879-1880 - Height 30 cm - Paris, Musée National du Louvre - *While still a young man, Degas discovered that the sculpture form was ideal for the expression of motion.*

XLIV - A Dancer at the Age of Fourteen - Bronze, 1880 - Height 98 cm - Paris, Musée National du Louvre - *This statuette of a young ballerina is complete with a cloth leotard and a tulle tutu. These sculptures helped Degas to understand the role of body movement and to use the knowledge in his paintings.*

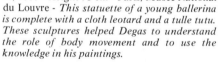 XLV - Grand Arabesque: Third Movement - Bronze - Height 42 cm - Paris, Musée National du Louvre - *The swiftly moving grace of the dancer is poised, in equilibrium, on a solid horizontal base.*

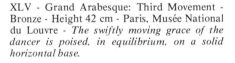  XLVI - The Green Singer - 1884 - New York, The Metropolitan Museum of Art, the Havemeyer Collection - *The unusual linear perspective, the positioning of the subject, and the play of light and shadow there combine to give an interesting effect of fantasy and realism.*

 XLVII - Women in Café - Paris, Musée National du Louvre, Cabinet des Dessins - *Women were a favorite subject of Degas and were used as a symbol of the colorful modern world around him, which never failed to stimulate his curiosity and inspire him.*

XLVIII - A Corner of the Stage during the Ballet - Private collection - *The imaginative quality of the ballet fascinated Degas. The wonderful world of make-believe-stage settings, costumes, lighting—had special meaning for him.*

XLIX - Ballerina Tying Her Shoe - Private collection - *Degas's works were not "art for art's sake". He always attempted to give his visual images the life, the individuality and the graceful dignity he felt they deserved.*

L - The Laundresses - Paris, Musée National du Louvre - *This typical Montmartre scene shows Degas's intense interest in even the most mundane aspects of everyday life.*

LI - Laundress - 1882 - Collection of Mr. and Mrs. Paul Mellon - *The laundress was a recurrent motif in Degas's work. Here he portrays her in unstylized realism, toiling through her day's work.*

LII - Portrait of Pagan, or Man with Cigar - Private collection - *For Degas, the portrait was the most effective means of combining formal studies of line with the psychological interest of the individual lines he saw around him.*

LIII - At the Millinery Shop: Woman Trying on a Hat - Private collection - *Degas's keen powers of observation never stopped supplying him with fresh images of daily life, especially those of women, in whom he found an infinity of nuance and expression.*

LIV - Woman Combing Her Hair - Paris, Musée National du Louvre - *This work emphasizes Degas's fascination with the nude female form and his preoccupation with capturing the line of a motion.*

LV - After the Bath: Woman Drying Her Neck - Paris, Musée National du Louvre, Cabinet des Dessins - *In this painting, full of the vitality of life, the model seems almost surprised at being caught in a private moment of her toilette.*

LVI - After the Bath - Private collection - *The many examples of women in intimate moments show the artist's sensitivity to gesture and movement as expressive of life's ever-changing quality.*

LVII - The Bath: Woman Drying Her Feet - Paris, Musée National du Louvre - *Degas's theme of women glimpsed in private moments owes as much to the traditional of Renaissance nudes as it does to Impressionism and painters like Renoir. Here the tautness of line is relieved and softened by the sensual use of color.*

LVIII - Portrait of Seated Woman - 1892-1895 - Paris, Private collection - *This pastel is an example of Degas's constant experimentation with new techniques in his later years. He considered pastels particularly versatile.*

LIX - Portrait of Alexis Ronart - 1895 - Private collection - *Degas was always meticulous, both in his large-scale works and in sketches dashed off quickly for friends, as in this pastel.*

LX - Russian Dancers - c. 1895 - Stockholm, Nationalmuseum - *This pastel demonstrates how the ever-evolving search for new techniques brought Degas to the point where even a simple outline sketch resembled the intricate weave of a cloth.*

LXI - Three Dancers in Violet Tutus - *Degas often utilized his pictures of dancers as exercises in testing new technical approaches and new ways of representing light and color.*

LXII - Three Dancers - Private collection - *By 1900, the date of this pastel, the painter's eyesight was rapidly deteriorating: yet this handicap seemed to spur him on to greater innovations and greater chromatic freedom in the use of light.*

LXIII - Blue Dancers - Paris, Musée National du Louvre - *In his final years Degas was totally caught up in the magic of color and his fascination with movement and linear perspective took on an almost absolute importance. The human figure finally became merely a vehicle.*

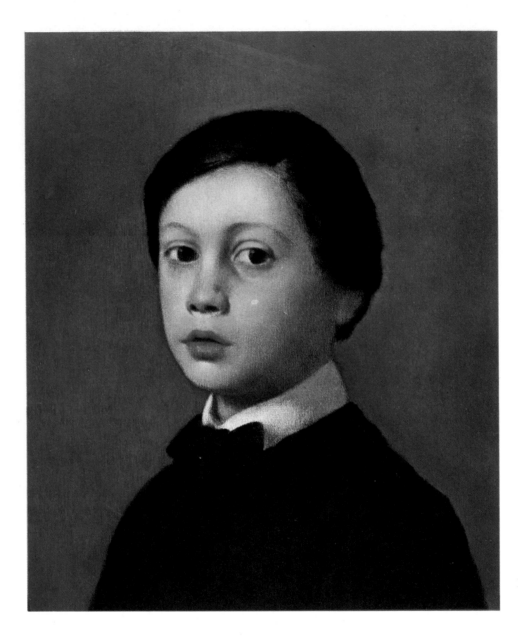

IV

VIII

XII

XIV

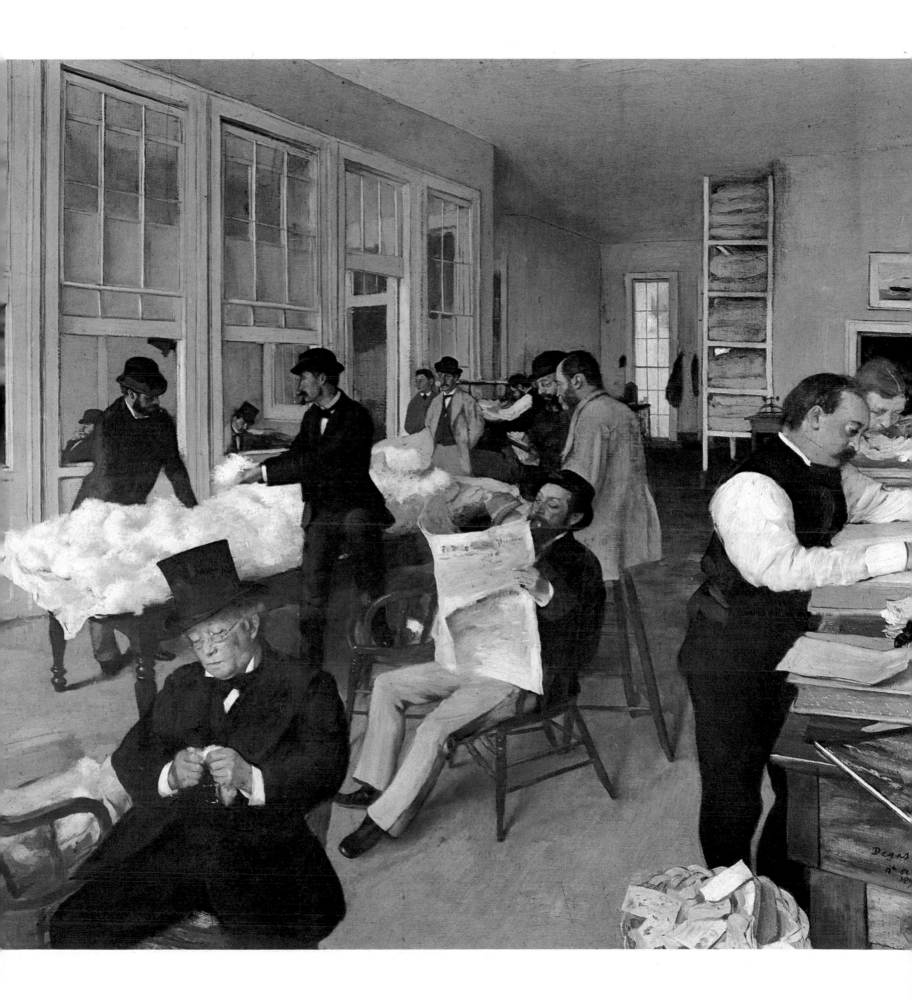

XVIII

XXII

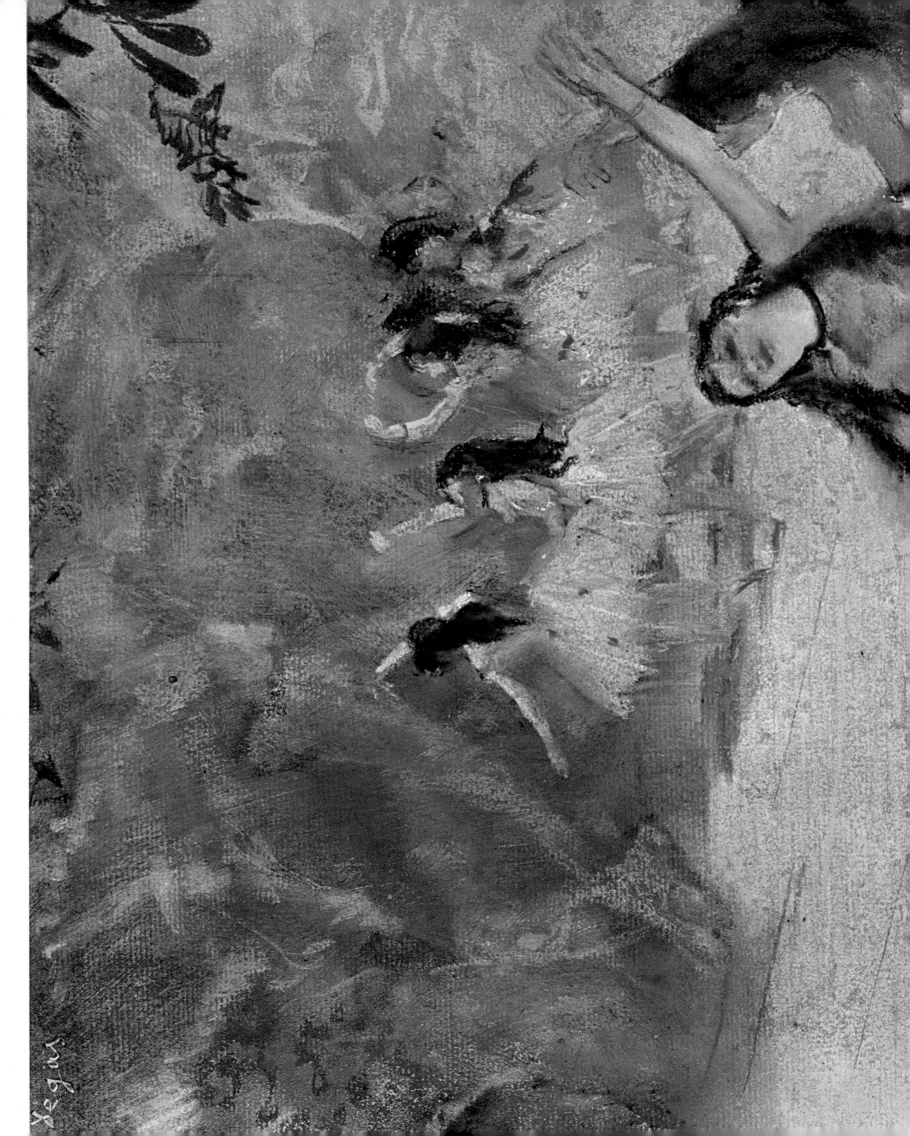

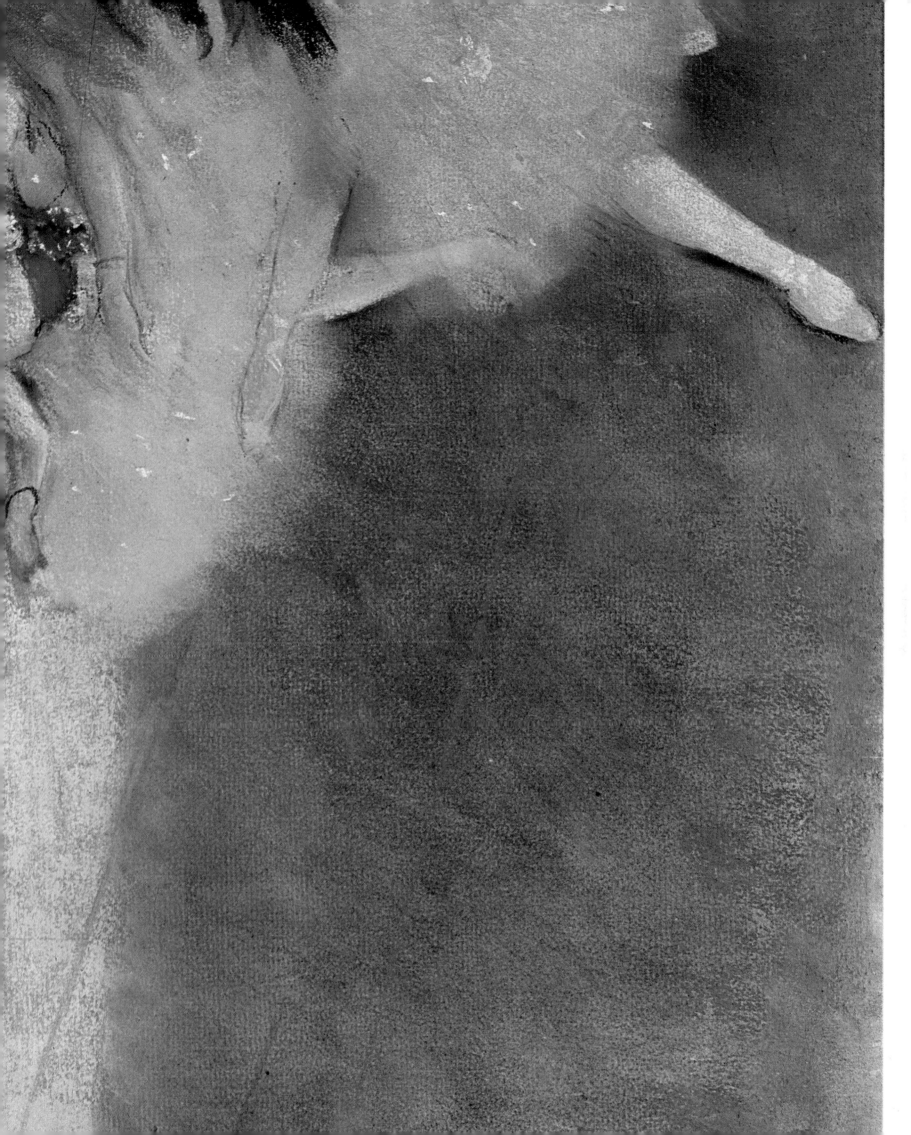

XLII

XLVI

XLVIII

Degas

XLIX

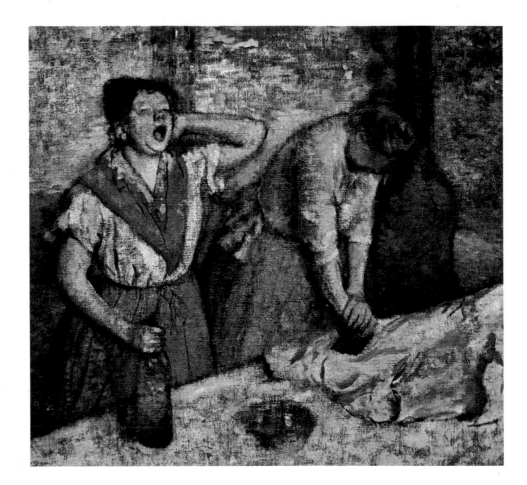

LIV

LVI

LVIII

Alexi Rouart
mars 1895

Degas

LIX

LX

LXII